Calgary

The City and Sights

HIGH COUNTRY COLOUR

Above: *Glenmore Resevoir*

Below: *Skyline at Dusk*

Above: *Calgary's Olympic Plaza*

Below: *Prince's Island Park with skyline in background*

Aerial view of Calgary with The Canadian Rockies in the background.

CONTENTS

CALGARY

· · · · · · · · ·

A BRIEF HISTORY

It was an atmosphere of general lawlessness that brought fifty members of the Northwest Mounted Police to southern Alberta in 1875. Independent fur traders were acting outside the authority of the Hudson's Bay Company, who was supposed to be in control of the lands of western Canada, then known as Rupert's Land. The independents were fighting over control of trading in buffalo hides, a highly valuable and popular commodity which helped fend off the cold North American winters. These traders would do anything they could to maintain control over the native people, who held the supply of buffalo furs. This control included locally processed "whiskey", which caused harm in two ways - the deadly ingre-

Above: One of the many sculptures that are located in Calgary.
Right: The downtown skyline with the Olympic Saddledome in the foreground.

dients and the violence which always seemed to result from its consumption.

The Northwest Mounted Police, under the direction of Colonel James Macleod, established a fort at the confluence of the Bow and Elbow Rivers. He named it "Fort Calgary" after his home in the Scottish Highlands. Almost immediately the fort attracted a small collection of tents and cabins close to its walls. Two stores, including one owned by the Hudson's Bay

Company, were built very quickly to capitalize on the growing population. What eventually become the City of Calgary was born.

The rapid decline in buffalo population due to overhunting caused the government to look for other ways to utilize the vast prairie lands and try to bolster its suddenly collapsing economy. It granted leases for up to 40,000 hectares of land for anyone willing to begin a cattle ranch.

Soon over 600,000 hectares of land were being grazed by thousands of head of cattle.

The railway arrived in 1883 causing another large influx of people and in 1884, with a population of 4000, the town of Calgary was officially created. In 1892 it became a city.

The early 1900's was a period of remarkable growth. Although Edmonton became the provincial capital in 1905, Calgary was booming. People speculating in

Left, top: Calgary is one of the premier places for hot air balloon enthusiasts in North America.
Left, bottom: The city skyline is a spectacular sight at night.
Below: A full moon keeps watch over the Calgary Tower as the city begins another busy day.

Right: The Armengol Sculptures, with their outstretched hands, are symbols of friendship and goodwill.

Below: There are many vantage points in Calgary where one can get a view of the mountains in the distance.

Next page: The light rail transit system, known as the C-Train, connects the downtown core with communities in the south and north.

Overleaf: Clear night air helps the buildings of downtown Calgary sparkle with light.

10

real estate became millionaires almost overnight as rumour after rumour of new and large businesses establishing themselves in Calgary flourished. Demand for housing was so high that many were forced to live in tents until their homes could be built. The meat packing industry was established and by 1912 the city had grown to a population of 45,000.

A 1914 oil discovery at Turner Valley, 50 kilometres southwest of Calgary further fueled the boom and some 500 new businesses were established. The city became Canada's oil capital, a title which it still holds today.

Previous page, bottom: Another beautiful sunset is reflected in the waters of the Bow River.
Left: These highly detailed horse sculptures are on display outside of the Municipal Building.
Below: The indoor Devonian Gardens in the downtown Toronto Dominion Square provide an oasis for busy office workers.

Right: The annual Calgary Stampede provides enjoyment for all including these native children dressed up in their colourful costumes.
Below: The midway rides at the Stampede attract thousands of people seeking excitement.
Next page: One of the best ways to get a view of the city is from the top of the Calgary Tower, or take a ride in a helicopter.

TODAY'S CALGARY

Today the city has a population of around 800,000 and, despite the perpetual ups and downs of the previous century, enjoys a net growth every year. It is still the oil capital with many of the head offices of Canada's oil companies located here. The beef industry does not dominate as it once did, but it is still a significant contributor to the local economy. In an effort to diversify the economy away from its oil and natural gas bases, the provincial and city governments have attracted many high tech and manufacturing concerns.

Although many Canadians think Calary's climate to be harsh, in reality it is quite moderate. Summers are warm and

Above: Calgary's large network of parks and pathways are often patrolled by police on horseback.
Right: Although the downtown core is not as large as many North American cities, Calgary enjoys a great variety of office building styles.

18

very sunny with occasional very hot days. Summer nights are almost always cool making it great for sleeping. Winter seems to come early with frost in September and the first cold snap often occurring in October, but that is deceiving since there can still be many more warm days extending into November. Occasional blasts of Arctic air send temperatures down into the minus 20's and 30's or more but those days just serve to increase

anticipation in one of southern Alberta's great miracles - the chinook. Warm, dry winds, having deposited their moisture in the Rockies, travel down the eastern mountain slopes and continue over the prairies raising temperatures by as much as 30 degrees in an hour, and sometimes back down just as quickly. Often, however, chinooks will blow for several days at a time bringing children and adults out of their winter cocoons to participate in any number of activities.

Calgary has many characteristics which have made it well-known around the world but the most recent activity that brought it international attention was the staging of the 1988 Olympic Winter Games. For over two weeks the city played host to the world's best athletes and many thousands of spectators. Many of the facilities put in place for the games are still in use like the

Previous page, top: The Centre for the Performing Arts is home to Theatre Calgary, one member of the city's active arts scene.
Previous page, bottom: The warm light of dawn shines on the downtown office buildings.
Below: The central route of the C-Train through downtown Calgary allows thousands of office workers to take advantage of its service.

Right: *The twin towers of Western Canadian Place are two of the many beautiful buildings in the downtown area.*
Below: *Beautiful skies are one of the bonuses of living in or visiting Calgary.*
Next page: *There are many vantage points to enjoy a view of downtown.*

Speedskating Oval and the Saddledome where the National Hockey League's Calgary Flames play. The Olympic Games are a time that no citizen of Calgary will ever forget.

The Calgary Stampede

*P*erhaps no annual event is more anticipated than the Calgary Stampede. Every year for the first two weeks in July, cowboys of the real and drugstore variety descend on the city for one giant non-stop party.

The Stampede was the invention of Guy Weadick who responded to the public's desire to see and learn more about the life of the cowboy and for the true cowboys to partici-pate in competitions to show off their skills. He was able to convince four wealthy men that his dream was realistic and, with a donation of $100,000, the Calgary Stampede was born in 1912. It was staged again in 1919 and 1923 and its continued success resulted in it becoming an annual event beginning in 1924.

During the Stampede the city is transformed into a modern version

Above right: *Every afternoon cowboys compete for prize money.*
Above left: *The Chuckwagon races are very exciting event.*

of a western town. Every morning there are several free pancake breakfasts hosted by downtown businesses and there is lunchtime entertainment at "Rope Square" which is Olympic Plaza during the rest of the year. At the Stampede grounds cowboys complete with each other in various roping, riding and steer wrestling events every afternoon. Each evening there are chuckwagon races followed by a grandstand show of music and entertainment. This is all capped off by fireworks around 11 PM. For the adventurous, the midway offers an abundance of rides and other activities to test your skill and luck. Combine all of this with foods from around the world and it is easy to understand why visitors return frequently to enjoy the Stampede.

Previous page: The Stampede midway takes on a whole new personality after dark.

Above: The midway is very colorful during the day.

27

Above: *The highly entertaining chuck-wagon races take place every evening at the Stampede.*

Above: *The many buildings of the University of Calgary are located in the city's northwest.* **Left:** *The Olympic Oval was the site of the speed skating events at the 1988 Olympics.*

Previous page: The Olympic torch on top of the Calgary Tower is still occasionally lit to commemorate special events in the city.
Left: *The unique design of the Lindsay Park Sports Centre dominates this aerial photo of Calgary.*
Below: *Three ski jumps are located at Canada Olympic Park on the city's western edge.*

Previous page: The Olympic
Saddledome, named for its
distinctive shape, is home to
the National Hockey League's
Calgary Flames.
Left: The Burns Stadium is
home to the Calgary Cannons,
a minor league affiliate of the
Pittsburgh Pirates.
Below: McMahon Stadium,
site of the opening and closing
ceremonies of the 1988
Olympics, is home to the
Canadian Football League's
Calgary Stampeders.

ACTIVITIES FOR YOUNG AND OLD

Calgary is a city where lifestyle is important to its citizens. Every day you can see people running, walking or cycling along its extensive pathway system. Begun in 1973 these pathways now cover over 200 kilometres in length.

The city's proximity to the mountains has a profound effect on people. In winter the ski areas of Fortress Mountain, Nakiska, Lake Louise, Sunshine and Mount Norquay draw thousands of active families to their slopes. In the summer hikers head off on many hundreds of kilometres of marked trails for one or multi-day excursions.

Above: Many different types of art work, including sculptures, can be found in Devonian Gardens.
Right: As this aerial photograph shows, the city has grown considerably in its one hundred year history.

There is much to do without ever leaving the city. Skiing, for example, begins in November at Canada Olympic Park on the city's western edge. Hiking takes place in many places but three favourites are Nose Hill in the north, Weaselhead Flats in Glenmore Park in the city's southwest and Fish Creek Provincial Park, also in the southwest. Fishing is a perpetual activity along the banks of the Bow River at dozens of locations. Sailors

head on to the Glenmore Reservoir in the summer months. Golf can be enjoyed at any number of local courses.

Calgary's past can be explored in great detail at the Glenbow Museum. If you want to experience the past close-up, then head to Heritage Park where many of the city's turn of the century buildings and houses have been preserved. Many of the businesses, like the bakery and blacksmith shop, are still in operation.

Sports enthusiasts have much to choose from. The popular Calgary Flames play hockey in the Olympic Saddledome and fans enjoy a friendly and deep-rooted rivalry with the Edmonton Oilers. The Calgary Cannons play at Burns Stadium. The Canadian Football League's Calgary Stampeders are based out of McMahon Stadium. Minor hockey, little league baseball and soccer keep parents and kids hopping all year round.

Previous page, top: At night the lights of the Calgary Tower can be seen for many miles.
Previous page, bottom: Although the Calgary Tower does not dominate the skyline as it once did, its distinctive shape is well known throughout the world.
Below: Diners in the Calgary Tower revolving restaurant are rewarded with a panoramic view that makes one complete turn every hour.

Right: The downtown Eaton Centre provides shoppers with a great variety of stores to choose from.
Below: The head office of AGT, the province's telephone company, is located in its own tower in downtown Calgary.
Next page: There are many places to enjoy a beautiful sunny afternoon in the downtown core.

Parks and Gardens

*B*ecause southern Alberta receives only a moderate amount of precipitation in an average year the prairie area around Calgary has a tendency to look rather brown by the end of the summer. Calgary itself, however, remains quite green thanks in part to its proximity to the Bow and Elbow Rivers but largely to the city's Parks and Recreation Department who are responsible for maintaining large amounts of park land throughout the city.

Those who enjoy Calgary's green spaces can thank William Pearce, a pioneer who encouraged the planting of trees, shrubs and flowers in an attempt to bring some colour to the dry prairie area that he lived in during the late 1880's. He was also instrumental in the development of the Calgary Irrigation Company which was responsible for piping

Above: *Devonian Gardens is home to over 20,000 native and tropical plants and is maintained at a constant temperature year round.*
Left: *The sunny summers of Calgary ensure the growth of colourful plants such as these Tiger Lilies.*

water to homes in Calgary making a gardener's job much less arduous.

Calgary is home to many very large public parks, some of which are actively maintained and some which are allowed to remain in a natural state. Bowness Park in the northwest part of the city is a wonderful example of a multi-use, all-season park. In the summer, families wander its pathways, enjoy a picnic beside the Bow River or rent small boats for use in the lagoon. In winter the lagoon freezes and is maintained as a skating rink with firewood provided to take the chill off the cold days. Riley Park in the southwest is a fine example of a well manicured park. Its flower gardens and trees provide wedding parties with a beautiful place for formal photographs; cricket matches are frequently played on its outdoor fields; and children enjoy countless hours of fun at the playground and in the wading pool.

Two of the best natural areas are the Weaselhead Flats area of Glenmore Park in the southwest and Nose Hill Park in the north. The Weaselhead area is where the Elbow River drains into the Glenmore Reservoir at the west end of Glenmore Park. In this area wildlife

Previous page: Weaselhead Flats, located at the western part of Glenmore Park, is a favorite spot of local residents. ***Above:*** *The waters of Glenmore Reservoir, seen here through the poplar trees of Glenmore Park, are a major source of Calgary's drinking water.*

such as deer and coyotes and the occasional moose are seen with many species of bird life. Informal pathways wind their way through-out the flats allowing people hours of exploration. Nose Hill is a real treat for nature lovers. It sits high on a hill with the best views of Calgary and the surrounding area that can be found. Its wide open spaces and prairie grasses gives one a sense of what it must have been like to live here a century or more ago.

If you want to feel "green" at any time of the year then head to the Devonian Gardens in downtown Calgary. It is located on the fourth floor of Toronto Dominion Square and is home to thousands of differ-ent plants and flowers. It is a popular place with office workers, not only for its beauty, but because it is connected to many office buildings by the 'Plus 15' system of above ground walkways.

Previous page: Water is a major factor in the beauty of the Devonian Gardens.
Left: Even during the chill of a winter's day, Devonian Gardens maintains its beauty.
Above: The colourful gardens at Riley Park in the city's northwest are part of the over 7000 acres of park land in the city.

Right: The old fire hall in downtown Calgary has been fully restored and is now home to a private business.
Below: Calgary is home to many Canadian head offices of oil companies.
Next page: The distinctive shape of Bankers Hall is one of the newer downtown office buildings.

SOCIAL AND CULTURAL LIFE

Calgarians are extremely lucky to have such a large variety of social and cultural activities to chose from.

The Calgary Centre for the Performing Arts is home to the Calgary Philharmonic Orchestra, Theatre Calgary, Alberta Theatre Projects plus several other smaller theatre and dance groups. Calgary Opera often performs at the Jubilee Auditorium located on the Southern Alberta Institute of Technology campus and Alberta Ballet, which is based out of both Calgary and Edmonton, tours extensively. Stage West entertains patrons in its 470 seat Broadway-style dinner

Above: One of the many life-like dinosaurs at Calgary Zoo's prehistoric park.
Right: Sailing enthusiasts are able to take advantage of the waters of Glenmore Park for an afternoon's recreation.

theatre and is often headlined by a well known TV or film personality. Lunchbox Theatre, located in one of the downtown office buildings, provides one act plays, musicals and comedies for lunch time entertainment. The city is also home to many other smaller first class theatre and dance companies.

Calgary enjoys a full network of cinemas which provide first run movie entertainment. It is also home to an Imax Theatre at the new Eau Claire Market. More

avante-garde films can be found at the Plaza and Uptown Theatres.

Those looking for a taste of the past can head to the Glenbow Museum where displays and their extensive archives can provide an education about the area's history. For an "up-close-and personal" look at our past, Heritage Park is a perfect place to spend a day. This is Canada's largest living historical village with many working displays about life as our pioneers knew it, including a fully functional blacksmith shop and bakery. Fort Calgary Historic Park is currently rebuilding the original fort that founded Calgary. There are also a multitude of displays in the Interpretive Centre. If you want a visit to the prehistoric past then drive 90 minutes north and east of the city to the Royal Tyrell Museum at Drumheller to see the world's largest display of dinosaur skeletons. Other museums of note are the Aero Space Museum,

Previous page, top: A Canadian Pacific Railway steam locomotive takes visitors on a tour of Heritage Park. *Previous page, bottom:* Guests arriving at Heritage Park have the option of taking this authentic trolley car from the parking lot to the main gate. *Below:* Heritage Park is home to many exhibits including this steam locomotive which has been retired from use.

53

Alberta Sports Hall of Fame, the Grain Academy, the Museum of the Regiments and the Naval Museum of Alberta.

Calgary is also home to several festivals which take place annually, like the Big Rocky Mountain Jamboree (country music), the International Children's Festival, the International Jazz Festival, Calgary Winter Festival, the Folk Festival, the Barbeque on the Bow plus the Esther Honens International Piano Festival and Competition which is held every four years. Equestrian events take place regularly at Spruce Meadows, located at the southern end of the city.

Previous page, top: This giant 'H' and a large model of an ax are located near the entrance to Heritage Park.

Previous page, bottom: The main entrance to Heritage Park is built to look like an old fort.

Left: The SS Moyie takes Heritage Park visitors on a paddle wheel tour of the Glenmore Reservoir.

Below: This aerial view shows Heritage Park's 250 acre site beside the Glenmore Reservoir.

The Calgary Zoo

*T*he Calgary Zoo, also known by its extended title of Calgary Zoo, Botanical Garden and Prehistoric Park, is one of the best ways to spend a day or several days while in Calgary.

The Zoo is located on St. George's Island, one of three islands in the Bow River that was donated by the federal government to the City of Calgary in 1908. It began life as St. George's Island Park which evolved, after the formation of the Calgary Zoological Society in 1928, into the Calgary Zoo. It opened to the public in 1929 with a small collection of animals and birds. Its progress in the past decades is remarkable and it is now known as one of the finest zoos in the world. As it has grown it has become a much more humane place as well. In the 1970's the zoo management began a "ban the bars"

Above: *A Siberian Tiger enjoys a quiet afternoon in the shade at the Calgary Zoo.*
Left: *One of the polar bears of the Calgary Zoo wanders beside his pool.*

campaign which has meant the construction of animal enclosures more closely resembling their wild habitats. It has successfully bred many endangered species and hosts ongoing educational programs for the general public.

The Prehistoric Park, opened in the early 1980's, is an eight acre area displaying life-size replicas of dinosaurs in their natural habitat. Extensive construction and model-building make it easy to forget that you are just a stone's throw from downtown and not living in prehistoric times.

The Botanical Gardens are really many gardens rolled into one large area. Outdoors, flowers bloom from early spring to late fall. Horticulturists ensure a great variety of plants are growing and try to change displays from one year to the next. People are encouraged to spend some quiet time on the well-manicured lawns and enjoy the surrounding beauty. Indoors, the gardens take on several different personae. There is a rain forest display, an arid garden and an area set aside for the butterfly gardens, where butterflies flit about, sometimes landing on people's colourful clothing. In another part, tropical birds fly freely around landing in lush trees and bushes.

Previous page: The old and the new - a dinosaur at the Zoo's Prehistoric Park with the city skyline in the background. *Above:* This swan is in no danger of becoming lunch to the prehistoric creatures of the Calgary Zoo.

To learn more about other cultures, head to the Tsuu T'ina Nation where you can view native historical sites and enjoy dance demonstrations among other activities, or go to the Calgary Chinese Cultural Centre which features a museum, a Chinese Library, exhibitions, and a restaurant.

Looking for a food experience? You can find a whole range of culinary delights from gourmet meals to small deli's serving 'traditional' Canadian fare or food from any one of a number of different countries.

Previous page: Every year the gardens of the Calgary Zoo become a mass of colour.
Left: This large bison and some of his relatives can be seen at the Calgary Zoo.
Above: The indoor buildings of the Dorothy Harvie Gardens at the Zoo show a variety of plants from tropical locations.

Right: Cattle farming and oil are important staples of the Alberta economy.
Below: Between the western edge of the city and the mountains are many thousands of acres of rolling farmland.
Next page: One of the oil refineries that are located in the southern Alberta area.
Following page: The Olympic flame of the Calgary Tower glows over the downtown buildings.